910.4
For

Fortamn, Jan

First to Sail the World
Alone: Joshua Slocum

FIRST TO SAIL THE WORLD ALONE: Joshua Slocum

by Jan Fortman

Illustrated by
Gerald Smith

cpi
contemporary perspectives, inc.

This book is distributed by Silver Burdett Company, Morristown, New
Jersey, 07960.

Library of Congress Number: 78-13720

Art and Photo Credits

Cover illustration, Gerald Smith
Photos on page 48, The Peabody Museum of Salem.
Every effort has been made to trace the ownership of all copyrighted
material in this book and to obtain permission for its use.

Library of Congress Cataloging in Publication Data

Fortman, Janis L 1949-
    First to Sail the World Alone: Joshua Slocum.

    SUMMARY: Describes the voyage of Capt. Joshua Slocum, a 51-
year-old sailor, who in 1895 became the first man to sail around the
world alone in a 37-foot sloop that he rebuilt by hand.
    1. Voyages around the world — Juvenile literature. 2. Spray (Sloop)
— Juvenile literature. 3. Slocum, Joshua, b. 1844 — Juvenile literature. [1. Voyages around the world. 2. Spray (Sloop) 3. Slocum,
Joshua, b. 1844] I. Title.
0440.S636F67   910'41'0924   [B]   78-13720
ISBN 0-89547-054-3

Manufactured in the United States of America
ISBN 0-89547-054-3

Contents

Chapter 1

I Thought I Was Alone

Joshua Slocum lay helpless on the floor of the cabin. He had a fever so terrible that he could not stand up. His face was deathly white and his head was spinning. He knew he was not just seasick. He had sailed too many years not to know what *that* felt like. No, Joshua Slocum knew he had somehow been poisoned!

He was sick and all alone. And the ocean was wild, as heavy rain poured down. Slocum was aboard the small boat he was trying to sail around the world — all by himself. And now that boat rocked and tossed in the huge waves. *I can't control the boat*, Slocum thought. *And with no one to guide it, I'll sink in the storm.* His dream of being first to sail around the world alone would sink with him.

Hours passed. Somehow the boat stayed afloat. Slocum finally awoke from his fever. He looked out at the dark, stormy night. Great waves still smashed at the boat. Water poured over the deck. Looking out into the storm, Slocum suddenly gasped. Was he seeing something — or *someone* — on deck? Could that be a man standing at the wheel?

He, or *it*, looked like a pirate wearing a red cap. No, he looked more like the sailors Slocum had seen in old paintings. Slocum could not believe his eyes! Who was this man steering the boat? Was he real? Or did he live only in Slocum's fever? Slocum was too weak to stand up and find out.

The storm roared. Joshua Slocum closed his eyes. He thought of his round-the-world sail. The dream now seemed to have brought him to a certain death. He let the dream flash before his eyes once more.

Chapter 2

Was That a Ghost?

Joshua Slocum remembered building the boat with his own two hands. He had rebuilt it from the shell of an old boat. Board by board, nail by nail, he had put it together. It had taken him over a year to saw, fit, hammer, and paint it. And now, after all those months of hard work, the *Spray* was finally ready.

In his mind's eye, he remembered the day the boat was finished. He saw himself — a short, spry old man, sitting on a tree stump that day in the middle of a field. The smell of spring was in the air. Flowers were just pushing up out of the ground. And the buds on the cherry and apple trees were ready to burst.

Joshua Slocum too was about to burst. Every bone in his thin body tingled with excitement. He was about to begin the greatest adventure of his life — maybe anyone's life. And his new boat, the *Spray*, would be the key to whether or not he could live through the adventure.

The *Spray* was a 37-foot sailboat. It was all white with "*SPRAY*" painted in black letters on its side and back.

"No one has ever sailed around the world alone. I can't see why. People may say I'm just a crazy old man, but I know I can do it!"

Joshua Slocum was 51 years old when he finished building the *Spray*. He was born on February 20, 1844, in Nova Scotia, Canada. He came from a family of sailors and fell in love with the sea when he was a boy. But, like many sailors, he had never learned to swim.

By the age of 26, Slocum was the captain of a great sailing ship. His ship carried cargo to such lands as Australia, the Orient, and the Spice Islands. His travels had taken him around the world five times by sail — but never alone. No one had ever done that. Perhaps no one ever would. Others had tried. But Joshua Slocum felt sure he would be the first to make it.

It was noon, on April 24, 1895, when Joshua Slocum set out in the *Spray*. The skies were sunny and the wind was good for sailing. As the *Spray* slipped out

of Boston harbor, people waved at Slocum and wished
him a safe voyage.

Slocum gazed at the vast blue ocean stretched out
ahead of him. His heart was beating fast. He was
thrilled to be at sea again, breathing in the cold, crisp
air. He smiled when he saw a small rainbow out in
front of the boat. *A sailor's good luck sign!*

And so, Joshua Slocum set out to live his dream. But
as brave as his words had been he now found himself
wondering why he wanted to make this lonely sail.
Would he ever see his home again?

Slocum had now been at sea for three months. Most
of the time the weather had been good. He just sat
back and enjoyed the sail. The day before, he had
stopped at an island in the Azores. He had picked
some fresh fruit there — some plums. Now, as he lay
sick in his boat, he remembered eating a plum with a
piece of white cheese. Soon after that the cramps and
fever began.

Slocum felt the boat rolling under him. The storm
had not let up. And he was still burning with fever. He
felt so sick that even death by drowning might not be
worse. Slowly Slocum opened his eyes. He could still

see that strange, ghostly figure with a red cap. He still stood at the wheel!

Suddenly, the figure turned to Slocum and called out to him. The voice seemed to float on the wind. "I am the pilot of the *Pinta*. I have come to help you. I will guide your boat tonight."

Slocum pulled himself to his feet. He held on to the cabin wall to stand. The old sailor was amazed. The pilot of the *Pinta!* The *Pinta* had been one of Columbus's ships — 400 years ago! The ghost with the red cap spoke again. "Never eat plums with that kind of white cheese. If you do, you will become very ill."

"It's too late to tell me that now!" Slocum yelled. He had to shout to be heard above the roar of the storm. "Are you some sort of fool? Why would you want to sail in such weather?"

The ghostly sailor just laughed and began to sing. Slocum could hear the man's singing even over the sound of the storm. Slocum slid back to the cabin floor. There, he fell into a dream-like state. He felt crazy with fever. But he slept all night.

When he finally awoke it was morning. The storm was over, and the sea was calm again. Slocum felt much better. He quickly looked at his charts to find out how far off course the boat had been thrown.

Amazingly, the *Spray* had stayed on course all through the night! What was more, it had traveled 90 miles in the storm! Then Slocum remembered the ghostly sailor from the *Pinta*. Was it a dream? Had he actually been saved by a talking, singing ghost? He would never know for sure.

By the time the storm was over, Joshua was looking at a wonderful sight. All the birds were flying in the same direction. This was a sign land was near. Sure enough, when the clouds began to break, Slocum spotted some sunlit land on the far horizon. It was the coast of Spain!

Slocum headed for the Strait of Gibraltar, between southern Spain and North Africa. His plan was to sail east — through the Mediterranean Sea. He pulled the *Spray* into a Spanish port near San Fernando. There he could pick up food and cooking fuel, which he badly needed.

He talked with many people about his sailing plan. They warned him to stay away from the Mediterranean. It was crawling with pirates. He would be lucky to get through it alive.

Slocum did not have to be warned twice! He had heard much in his lifetime at sea about the pirates of the Mediterranean. They had fast ships and many sails. It was said that they could overtake any boat on the water. And the pirates themselves were ruthless criminals. They were without honor, without mercy. What should he do?

That evening, as he went to sleep, he felt something strange. Was that a tap on his arm? How could it be? He was alone on his boat. He looked around the dark cabin. And then he saw *him* again. Or was it a dream? It was the ghost of the sailor from the *Pinta* — wearing the same red cap. He was saying, "Turn back, Joshua Slocum. Turn back!"

So Slocum sailed back the way he had come. He went back across the Atlantic Ocean. But this time he sailed southwest. He was moving toward the coast of South America, west of the Sahara Desert, through the Canary Islands.

A few days after he set sail from Spain, the sea was choppy again. Waves were starting to splash over the deck of the *Spray*. Suddenly, in the early morning sunlight, Slocum spotted a boat far behind him. It was moving much faster than the *Spray*. Soon Slocum could see it clearly.

What he saw made his blood run cold. The ship was flying a black and white Jolly Roger — the flag of a pirate ship! He had changed his course to keep away from pirates. But he had run into them anyway!

Slocum felt like a doomed man. What could he do? There was no way to outrace the pirates. Their ship was much faster than his. He had a gun. But there were so many of them on the ship he decided not to shoot. He wouldn't stand a chance.

But the great ocean, which can so quickly end a life, can also save one. Suddenly out of nowhere great waves smashed over the *Spray*. The little boat shook in every timber. The water poured over the deck, and Slocum hung on for his life. It seemed to him that the *Spray* was standing on end for just a moment.

The huge wave passed. Slocum looked back to see the pirate ship. The wave had turned it over! The pirates were swimming in the sea! He could see their heads bobbing in the waves as they swam for their overturned boat. His life had been saved by the giant wave!

Or did he have other help? The picture of an old sailor with a red cap flashed through his mind.

Slocum merely smiled, scratched his head, and sailed on.

NORTH AMERICA

NORTH

AMERICA

NORTH PACIFIC OCEAN

NOVA SCOTIA

BOSTON
NEW YORK

SABLE IS

NORTH

ATLANTIC

AZORES

GIBRALTAR

BERMUDA

MADIERA

CANARY IS

BAHAMAS

PUERTO RICO

OCEAN

CUBA

ANTIGUA

CAPE VERTE

TRINIDAD

EQUATOR

SOUTH

SOUTH

PERNAM BUCO

ASCENSION

MARQUESAS IS

PACIFIC

SOUTH

ST H

SAMOA

PACIFIC

AMERICA

RIO DE JANEIRO

SOUTH

OCEAN

ATLANTIC

CAPE OF

JUAN FERNANDEZ IS

MONTE VIDEO

OCEAN

BUENOS AIRES

FALKLAND IS

STRAIT OF MAGELLAN

TIERRA DEL FUEGO

CAPE HORN

EUROPE

ASIA

AFRICA

NORTH

PACIFIC

OCEAN

JAPAN

EQUATOR

SUMATRA

JAVA   TIMOR   NEW GUINEA

KEELING OR
COCOS IS

COOKTOWN

RODRIGUEZ   SAMOA

BOWEN   FIJI

PORT NATAL
(DURBAN)

MADAGASCAR   AUSTRALIA

CAPE
TOWN   AUSTRALIA

INDIAN OCEAN

NEW CASTLE   SOUTH

SYDNEY

MELBOURNE

NEW ZEALAND

TASMANIA   LAUNCESTON

PACIFIC

A CHART OF
The "Spray's" Voyage
AROUND THE WORLD
24th April, 1895 ~ 27th June, 1898

OCEAN

Chapter 3

A Boat
Out of Water

To those who sail the seas, the ocean is not a flat plain without features. Like the land, its different areas are plainly marked. But not with valleys, forests, and deserts. No, the ocean is marked by the changing moods of its weather. There are great stretches of water that always seem calm. And there are others where there are unending storms.

But there are also parts of the ocean that sailors can never count on. Sometimes they will be calm and peaceful. Other times, a sudden storm will spring up, carried by winds that seem to blow from every direction at once.

One such part of the Atlantic is called the *doldrums*. Just north of the equator, the doldrums are waters that lie between the northern and southern *trade winds*.

The ocean is usually calm in this area. But sudden changing winds can whip up a storm at just about any time! The *Spray* was sailing through the doldrums about 1,500 miles west of Africa and about 1,000 miles east of French Guiana. The winds began to whirl and shift.

One moment the wind came from the northwest. Then suddenly it would come from the east. Often it was impossible to tell *where* the wind was coming from. It seemed to be coming from everywhere at once! The blue skies gave way to black. Rain poured down one minute and stopped the next. The wind began to howl.

Then, just as suddenly as they began, the winds died down. There was no breeze for hours. The *Spray* sat still, her sails limp. And Slocum was helpless. He could do nothing but wait for the wild winds to pick up again and start tossing his boat around.

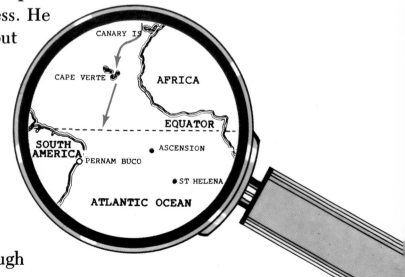

It went on that way for ten days. Slowly the *Spray* made its way through the doldrums. Finally Slocum was sailing once again on a smooth blue ocean. The *Spray*, its sails full, was pushed along by a strong wind. Slocum could see land in the distance. This time it was the coast of South America.

One night the ocean current was strong and running north. But Slocum was moving south. He had to keep the *Spray* close to the shore where the water moves more slowly. The bright moon made it hard to tell where the land met the sea. Slocum found it hard to see the shore. And he ran the *Spray* right onto the beach!

The old sailor knew he had to work fast. The tide was going out. He had to get the heavy anchor off the boat. Soon there wouldn't be any water under the boat. If he was going to get off the beach he would have to make the *Spray* as light as possible.

He untied the lifeboat. He dropped the heavy anchor and lines into it. He would row the anchor into deeper water and drop it. But the lifeboat wasn't made to hold so much weight. It began to leak. Joshua rowed as hard and as fast as he could.

Finally Slocum thought he was far enough away from the shore. But the lifeboat was starting to sink! There was no time to lose. With all his strength he threw the heavy anchor into the water. The sudden

movement caused the lifeboat to turn over. Slocum was thrown into the surf! He grabbed for the side of the boat. He was not that far from the beach. But he needed to hang on to the boat. He didn't know how to swim!

Splashing about in the water, Slocum tried to turn the lifeboat over. First he pushed too hard. The lifeboat rolled all the way over! Again Slocum tried, and again he failed. There was no way he was going to get back into that boat. But then he felt the boat stop rocking. He pulled down on one side. The boat turned over easily. It was almost as if . . . as if someone else were on the other side of the boat *helping* him.

Slocum climbed into the boat and paddled to shore. But all the while he rowed, he found himself looking out into the dark. *Was the ghost of a 400-year-old sailor wearing a red hat somewhere out there?*

When Slocum finally crawled onto the beach it was morning. The warm sun was beating on his tired body. He lay down behind a sand dune. Hidden from the wind, he fell asleep.

Suddenly he was awakened by the sound of a horse galloping on the beach. The horse stopped on top of the dune that hid Slocum. The old sailor looked up. His heart was filled with fear. This was wild country. Slocum didn't know if the people were friendly.

24

A young boy sat on the horse. The boy didn't see Slocum. But he did see the *Spray* sitting on the beach. The boy rode over to the boat and tied his horse to it. He was trying to get the horse to drag the boat. But it was much too heavy. Slocum watched for a while, smiling at the sight. Finally he came out from behind the dune and spoke.

"I would like to trade some biscuits for fresh eggs and milk." He pointed to the food in the boat and made some signs until he was sure the boy understood.

At first the boy was surprised to see the stranger. Then his face lit up with a smile. He jumped onto his horse and rode away. Soon he returned — with butter, milk, eggs, and many people.

When the tide came in, two men helped Slocum float the *Spray* out to sea. With another adventure behind him, he could relax and look forward to what tomorrow would bring. And if Joshua Slocum was sure of anything as he sailed south, it was that he would find more adventure.

The *Spray* was headed for Cape Horn — some of the most terrible sailing waters in the world.

Chapter 4

Sailing the Cape With Some Carpet Tacks

In February the *Spray* reached the southern tip of South America, sailing around Tierra del Fuego, Argentina. Slocum was at Cape Horn. It is one of the most dangerous places in the ocean. He would have to take his boat through a narrow, rocky channel. A mistake on his part, or a shift in the wind, and the *Spray* could crash to pieces.

The sea at Cape Horn is always rough and the sky is black. Rocks lie hidden everywhere beneath the water. A strong wind blows without stopping all year round. It flings the water onto the rocky coast of South America, sending a white spray high into the air. Giant waves crash against the rocks.

No one knows how many lives have been lost rounding the Cape. Big, well-equipped ships have been splintered like matchsticks. In Slocum's day, it was a graveyard of sailing ships.

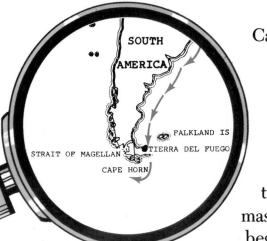

Sailing around Cape Horn alone in a small ship was the most impossible task that Slocum faced. He took his sails down, tied them to the mast, and carefully began to steer the *Spray* through the channel.

That night the ever-changing wind shifted and started to blow from the northwest. It was hitting the *Spray* head-on. With the changing winds came heavy rains. The strong winds roared, and the waves crashed against the boat and the rocky shore.

The winds were strong for 30 hours. Joshua stood at the wheel. He was tired to the point of falling over. And he was chilled to the bone. It took every ounce of strength to keep the *Spray* from smashing against the rocks.

The next day, when the wind was easier, Slocum found a sandy beach. He anchored and went ashore. He walked to a small village where he could buy supplies. While talking with the sailors in town, Slocum learned of some dangers of Cape Horn that had nothing to do with the sea or the rocks.

"As you move around the Cape you may run across some of the natives. They are cruel — killers, all of them," one old seaman told Slocum.

There was something about the sailor's voice that made Slocum listen and something about the man's eyes. *Where had he seen this man before? Where had he heard that voice?*

Before Slocum could answer his own thoughts, the sailor handed him a small, heavy bag.

"Take this bag. It will help if the natives should bother you."

"But these are only carpet tacks!" Slocum said, looking in the bag. He laughed. "What do I need these for?"

The old sea dog never even smiled at Slocum's question. He only said, "They will come in handy. Wait and see. But be careful — don't step on them!"

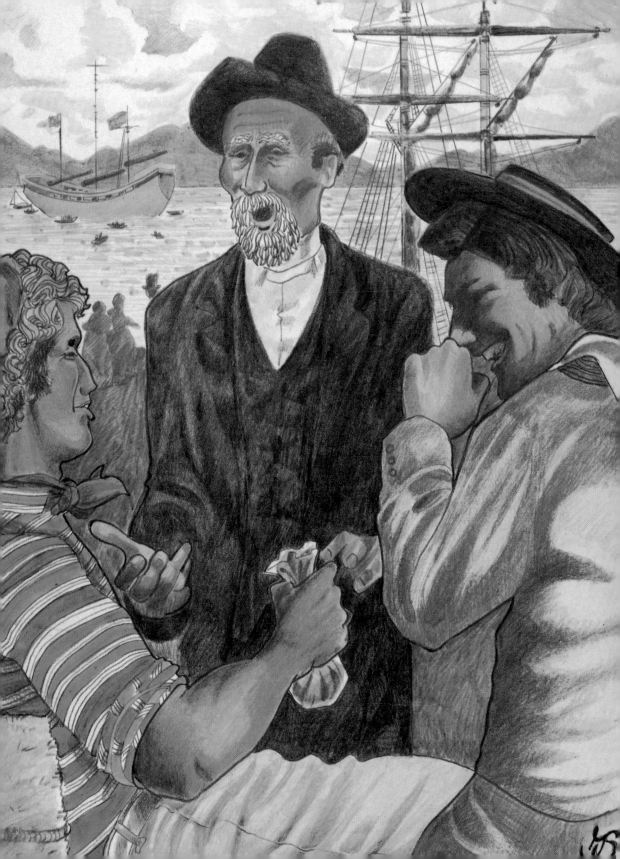

Slocum thought his voice sounded like that of the sailor in the red cap.

Another sailor told Slocum some terrible stories about natives attacking boats passing through the Cape. "The natives surround you in canoes. Shoot straight at them. Try to scare them, but don't kill them!"

Slocum thanked them and started to leave. He wanted to set sail while there were still a few hours of daylight.

"And watch out for the williwaws!" the old sailor called. "The williwaws are sudden, wild winds. They are so strong they can turn a ship over on its side. Be careful. They come when you least expect them."

Slocum tipped his hat and nodded. He put the bag of tacks in his coat pocket. He turned back as he heard the old sailor call out once more.

"And remember — don't step on the tacks!" yelled the old sailor. It was then that Slocum saw it. The old sailor was wearing a red cap!

Chapter 5

The Natives Attack

It was February 20th, 1896 — Joshua Slocum's birthday. It was ten months since he had left home, and he was now sailing around the southern tip of South America. So far he had seen no natives. But he knew they were nearby. He saw their fires on the shore light up the dark sky each night.

And he had an eerie feeling as he fought the rough water through the channel. Somehow he knew he was being watched all the time. He felt the natives were waiting to see what would happen. It was almost as if they were waiting to see if the ocean would take care of Slocum before they did.

Mostly, Slocum did not have time to worry about the natives. It took all his strength to battle the williwaws and fight the strong ocean current. Besides, he would soon be around the Cape and sailing the Pacific. If he could make the trip quickly enough, he would soon be far away from any danger the natives might cause him.

Soon the winds became too strong for sailing. Slocum had to anchor the *Spray* in a cove. When the sky cleared after several hours and the winds died down, he took up the anchor and set sail again.

He had been sailing for less than an hour when he saw the natives. Suddenly, their canoes were all around him. Slocum figured they had spotted him when he sailed out of the cove. The natives called to him. He didn't understand their words. But the meaning was clear. He could tell they wanted to board the *Spray*.

"No!" he yelled. He tried to wave them back with his arms. But the canoes kept coming closer. Slocum was trembling. He reached into the cabin for his gun. Remembering the sailor's advice, Joshua carefully aimed his gun straight at one canoe and shot at the boat, but not the people in it. He barely missed one of the natives. All the canoes quickly moved away.

For several days Slocum sailed the *Spray* between bare rocky islands — Navarino, Hermites, Hoste, and many more. He was slowly making his way through

the narrow channel. Few fish or birds seemed to visit this place. All he had heard for day after gloomy day was the roar of the wind and the crashing of waves.

At last the *Spray* cleared the islands of Londonderry and Stewart near the end of the channel. Stretched out before him lay the huge Pacific Ocean. Tired as he was, Slocum was filled with joy at the sight of the great ocean calling him forward. But the happy sailor did not know the ocean in this part of the world. The waters of Cape Horn were not finished with Joshua Slocum just yet.

No sooner had Slocum spotted the blue Pacific than the wind switched direction again. A storm came from out of nowhere. All at once, the *Spray* was drenched with rainwater. The northwest wind was so strong that Slocum couldn't make any headway. He was forced to sail southeast, back toward Cape Horn — back the painful way he had just come! And the storm showed no sign of lifting.

That night the sea was rougher than Slocum had ever seen it. The *Spray* was like a leaf on a tumbling stream. It was rocked and tossed every which way. Even Joshua Slocum, an old, lifelong sailor, could not fight off seasickness that night! Could it be that the high wind and Cape Horn would now beat him? Would the *Spray* become one more sunken tombstone in the underground graveyard of Cape Horn?

Finally the morning light showed through the clouds. Slocum dropped anchor near some sheltered islands. Tired and hungry, he ate some hot stew and rested. He was so tired that he knew he would sleep soundly. He lay down in the cabin and closed his eyes.

But sleep would not come. The tired sailor kept feeling someone, or *something*, trying to reach him. A voice? Yes, that was it! A voice that seemed to be saying, "Don't forget the tacks." Slocum went up and spread the carpet tacks all over the deck. Then he went below again. The gentle rocking of the boat lulled him quickly to sleep.

Hours later, when it was well after dark, Slocum was awakened by yelling and screaming on deck. Peering out of his cabin, he saw that a group of natives had come aboard and stepped on the tacks! As Slocum watched, the whole group jumped into the water and scrambled away in their canoes.

"So the tacks came in handy, after all!" Slocum said to himself. "Funny how the idea to spread them on the deck came to me that way."

The next day the weather was good, and the *Spray* was again moving through the narrow, rocky channel. When he reached the end of the Cape this time, Slocum anchored in a cove. There he repaired his

One night Slocum was surprised by the splashing and snorting of a huge whale.

small boat and mended the sails. He had proved himself to the sea. He had won over wind, wave, rock, and storm. Now, at last, the big Pacific Ocean welcomed him.

40

Chapter 6

Catching the Pacific Winds

The trade winds pushed the *Spray* for many thousands of miles. They took her all the way from Cape Horn to Australia. Joshua reached Australia in October. He spent nearly eight months there, sailing from port to port.

One night, while Slocum was below in his cabin, he heard a loud snorting outside. He ran onto the deck and found himself covered with water as a surprised whale turned around and splashed the ocean

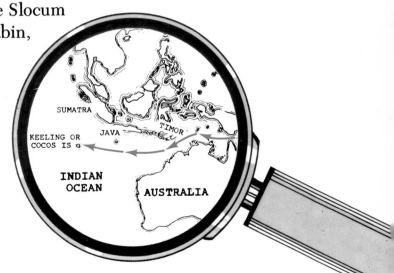

with its huge tail. The big sea mammal had nearly crashed into the *Spray!*

He sailed north and west, through the Indian Ocean. He stopped at islands all along the way. And at every one of these stops people wanted to know all about his trip. They were amazed that he was really sailing alone.

Soon the *Spray* was heading for the Cape of Good Hope at the southern tip of Africa. Strong trade winds kept the *Spray* moving at top speed.

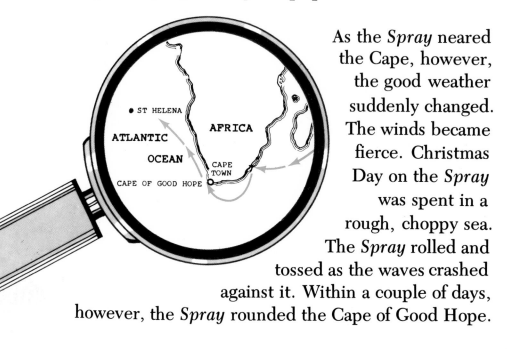

As the *Spray* neared the Cape, however, the good weather suddenly changed. The winds became fierce. Christmas Day on the *Spray* was spent in a rough, choppy sea. The *Spray* rolled and tossed as the waves crashed against it. Within a couple of days, however, the *Spray* rounded the Cape of Good Hope.

Slocum spent a few months in Capetown, South Africa, while his boat was tied up for repairs. He set

Slocum had many peaceful days aboard the *Spray.*▶

sail again in March. This time he headed west across the Atlantic.

A strong southeast wind pushed the *Spray* across the ocean. Porpoises and dolphins followed the boat each day. They were good company on the lonely sail. And great fun. They leaped clear out of the water. Their wet, graceful bodies shone in the sun. They were soon joined by flying fish. They jumped up and out of the water with their backs arched. And then they would gracefully dive back in.

On May 8, 1898, Slocum checked his chart and his old clock to figure his position. He had done this every day for more than three years. But today was different. As he bent over the charts Slocum suddenly shouted to the ocean, "I did it! I have circled the world!"

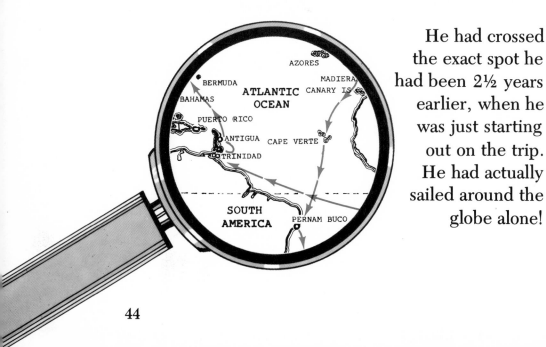

He had crossed the exact spot he had been 2½ years earlier, when he was just starting out on the trip. He had actually sailed around the globe alone!

"Soon I'll be home!" Slocum yelled to the fish swimming along with the *Spray*.

But to the end, the sea wouldn't give up to Joshua Slocum. Now, like a teasing friend, the ocean breeze suddenly stopped blowing. Slocum was just off the east coast of the United States. Her sails limp, the *Spray* sat in the smooth water like a sleeping bird. For eight days, the *Spray* remained almost in place. It hardly moved at all. Slocum could do nothing but wait for the wind.

At 1:00 A.M. on June 27, 1898, Slocum proudly sailed into the harbor at Newport, Rhode Island. It was three years and two months since he had set sail.

Joshua Slocum was in good health. So was the *Spray*. She hadn't leaked a single drop the entire trip around the world.

I said there wasn't any reason why I couldn't do it. Slocum thought as he sailed into the harbor. And just then he heard a voice singing. It sounded to him as it had in a storm almost three years ago. He had been sick with fever that night, but now he was not. Yet, as he looked out over the dark waters of home, he could still see a man's face smiling at him. It was the face of a 400-year-old sailor, still wearing a red cap. He was singing a song. And somehow Joshua Slocum, the

54-year-old man who had just sailed around the world, was certain of one thing.

Another world explorer by the name of Christopher Columbus had heard that same song.

Slocum, aboard his sloop *Spray*, set out to sail around the world in 1895.

Nine years after his lone sail around the world Joshua Slocum, then 60 years old, was still a man of the sea.